You Can't Be A Smart Cookie, If You Have A Crummy Attitude

by John C. Maxwell

Honor Books
Tulsa, Oklahoma

Merry Christmas to One Smart Cookie! Happy 1998!

3rd Printing
Over 65,000 in Print

You Can't Be A Smart Cookie,
 If You Have A Crummy Attitude
ISBN 1-56292-105-3
Copyright © 1995 by John C. Maxwell
1530 Jamacha Road, Suite D
El Cajon, California 92019

Published by Honor Books
P.O. Box 55388
Tulsa, Oklahoma 74155

INTRODUCTION

Attitude . . .

It is the "advance man" of our true selves.
Its roots are inward but its fruit is outward.
It is our best friend or our worst enemy.
It is more honest and more consistent than our words.
It is an outward look based on past experiences.
It is a thing which draws people to us or repels them.
It is never content until it is expressed.
It is the librarian of our past.
It is the speaker of our present.
It is the prophet of our future.

These quotes and insights have been gleaned from a lifetime of positive thinking and learning. I found out a long time ago that maintaining a positive mental attitude is the key to personal success in life. Read, learn, and file these ideas. Then go out and live them.

John C. Maxwell

John Maxwell

You are only an attitude away from success!
John Maxwell

The highest reward for man's toil is not what he gets for it but what he becomes by it.

John Ruskin

It's not whether you get knocked down, it's whether you get up.

Vince Lombardi

All our dreams can come true –
if we have the courage
to pursue them.
Walt Disney

In the middle of difficulty
lies opportunity.

Albert Einstein

The successful man will profit from his
mistakes and try again in a different way.

Dale Carnegie

What lies behind us and what lies before us are tiny matters compared to what lies within us.

Walt Emerson

I may not be able to change the world I see around me, but I can change the way I see the world within me.

Your attitude determines your action. Your action determines your accomplishment.

John Maxwell

We cannot direct the wind. . .
but we can adjust
the sails.

If you think you are beaten, you are.
If you think you dare not, you don't.
If you'd like to win but think you can't,
It's almost certain you won't.

Life's battles don't always go
To the stronger or faster man,
But sooner or later, the man who wins
Is the man who thinks he can.

A successful man is one who can lay a firm foundation with the bricks others have thrown at him.

David Brinkley

If things go wrong, don't go with them.

Roger Babson

You are today where your thoughts have brought you; you will be tomorrow where your thoughts take you.

James Allen

Winning is not everything –
but making the effort to win is.

Vince Lombardi

You never achieve real success unless you like what you are doing.

Dale Carnegie

You and I do not see things as they are.
We see things as we are.

Herb Cohen

Whether you think you can or
think you can't –
you are right.

Henry Ford

I have learned that success is to be measured
not so much by the position that one has
reached in life as by the obstacles which one
has overcome while trying to succeed.

Booker T. Washington

Our attitude toward things is likely to be more
important than the things themselves.

A.W. Tozer

Happiness depends not upon things
around me, but on my attitude.
Everything in my life will
depend on my attitude.

Alfred A. Montapert

The quickest way to correct the other fellow's attitude is to correct your own.

King Vidor

It's your attitude, not your aptitude that will determine your altitude.

God chooses what we go through;
we choose how we
go through it.
John Maxwell

It is a fact that you project
what you are.

Norman Vincent Peale

Life is not a dress rehearsal.

John Maxwell

A pessimist is a person who,
regardless of the present,
is disappointed in the future.

Do not let what you cannot do interfere
with what you can do.

John Wooden

We cannot continually behave in a manner
that is inconsistent with the way
we see ourselves.

Quitting is a
permanent solution to a
temporary problem.

The greatest discovery of our generation is that human beings can alter their lives by altering their state of mind.

William James

There is no wrong side of the bed. We get up on the wrong side of our mind.

The greatest mistake
a person can make
is doing nothing.
John Maxwell

It is the eye that makes the horizon.

Ralph Waldo Emerson

Believe you are defeated, believe it long
enough, and it is likely to become a fact.

Norman Vincent Peale

What really matters is
what happens in us,
not to us.

Every man takes the limits of his own field of vision for the limits of the world.

Arthur Schopenhauer

As he thinketh in his heart, so is he.

Proverbs 23:7

Men may be measured
by their reactions
to life's inequities.

The environment you fashion out of . . .
your thoughts . . . your beliefs . . . your ideals
. . . your philosophy . . . is the only climate
you will ever live in.

Alfred A. Montapert

Health, happiness, and prosperity
are primarily mental.

Marian Ramsay

Life is formed from the inside out.
What I am inside determines the
issues in the battle of life.

Dr. William Hornaday

Very little is needed to make a happy life.
It is all within yourself – in your way
of thinking and attitude.

Fred Corbett

Man's greatness lies in his power of thought.

Blaise Pascal

Others can stop you temporarily,
but you're the only one who
can do it permanently.

John Maxwell

An optimist may see a light where there is none, but why must the pessimist always run to blow it out?

Michel De Saint-Pierre

Growl all day and you'll feel dog tired at night.

Man must cease attributing his problems to his environment, and learn again to exercise his will.

Albert Schweitzer

We lost because we told ourselves we lost.

Leo Tolstoy

Be careful for nothing, prayerful for
everything, thankful for anything.

Dwight L. Moody

Never look back unless you
want to go that way.

If a man has Limburger cheese on his upper lip, he thinks the whole world smells.

John Maxwell

I go at what I do as if there were nothing else in the world for me to do.

Charles Kingsley

Places and circumstances never
guarantee happiness. You must
decide within yourself
whether you want to be happy.

Robert J. Hastings

Failure is only the opportunity to
begin again more intelligently.
Henry Ford

Opportunity looks bigger
going than coming.

Action and feeling go together,
and by regulating the action, . . .
we can directly regulate the feeling.
William James

The quality of a person's life is in direct proportion to their commitment to excellence, regardless of their chosen field of endeavor.

Vince Lombardi

Events are less important than our responses to them.

John Maxwell

Always bear in mind that your own resolution to succeed is more important than any other one thing.

Abraham Lincoln

To live a long time and to enjoy life,
the unseen force for you to develop
is the proper attitude.

Alfred A. Montapert

The quality of an individual is reflected in
the standards they set for themselves.

Ray Kroc

The purpose of human life
is to serve, and to show
compassion and the
will to help others.
Albert Schweitzer

The man who acquires the ability
to take full possession of his own
mind may take possession of anything else
to which he is justly entitled.

Andrew Carnegie

Who is rich? He that rejoices in his portion.

Benjamin Franklin

Nothing is as hard as it looks;
everything is more rewarding than you
expect; and if anything can
go right it will and at the
best possible moment.

Maxwell's Law

I thank God for my handicaps,
for through them, I have found myself,
my work, and my God.

Helen Keller

Where there is no hope in the future, there
is no power in the present.

John Maxwell

There is no security
in this life,
only opportunity.
General Douglas Mac Arthur

Success is peace of mind in
knowing you did your best.

John Wooden

Anyone who stops learning is old, whether at
twenty or eighty. Anyone who keeps
learning stays young.

Henry Ford

Football games are generally won
by the boys with the
greatest desire.
Paul "Bear" Bryant

The attitude of the individual determines
the attitude of the group.

John Maxwell

If a man has done his best, what else is there?

General George S. Patton

The last of the human freedoms
is to choose one's attitude in any
given set of circumstances.

Victor Frankl
(survivor of Nazi concentration camp)

It is no exaggeration to say that a strong, positive self-image is the best possible preparation for success in life.

Dr. Joyce Brothers

Misery is an option!

Bumper Sticker

I expect the best and
with God's help will
attain the best.

Norman Vincent Peale

You never get ahead of anyone
as long as you try to
get even with them.

Maintaining the right attitude is easier than
regaining the right attitude.

I firmly believe that any man's finest hour –
his greatest fulfillment to all he holds dear –
is that moment when he has worked his
heart out in a good cause and lies exhausted
on the field of battle – victorious.

Vince Lombardi

Don't Let Yourself . . .
WORRY when you're doing your best.
HURRY when success depends on accuracy.
THINK evil of anyone until you have the facts.
BELIEVE a thing is impossible without trying it.

Aim for the highest.

Andrew Carnegie

Even a mistake may turn out
to be the one thing necessary
to a worthwhile achievement.

Henry Ford

Nothing can stop the man with the
right mental attitude from achieving his goal;
nothing on earth can help the man with the
wrong mental attitude.

W.W. Ziege

I'm not sure all happy people are generous,
but I've never seen a generous person
who wasn't happy.

Life is like baseball;
it's 95% mental and the
other half is physical.

Yogi Berra

If you want to change attitudes, start with a change in behavior. In other words, begin to act the part, as well as you can, of the person you would rather be, the person you most want to become. Gradually, the old, fearful person will fade away.

Dr. William Glasser

Attitudes determine actions.
You are not what you think you are.
What you think, you are!

Accept the challenges so that you may feel the exhilaration of victory.

General George S. Patton

People catch our spirit just like they catch our colds: by getting close to us.

Every man over forty is responsible
for [the disposition of] his face.
Abraham Lincoln

A happy person is not a person in a certain set of circumstances, but rather a person with a certain set of attitudes.

Hugh Downs

Instead of saying TGIF, say TGIT –
Thank God it's today!

Keep your face to the sunshine
and you cannot see the shadows.
Helen Keller

Afflictions color your life,
but you choose the color.

People don't care how much you know until
they know how much you care.

John Maxwell

Sales are not made or unmade inside the prospect's office. They are made or unmade inside you.

Brian Azar

Wars may be fought with weapons, but they are won by men. It is the spirit of the men who follow and of the man who leads that gains victory.

General George S. Patton

It is unfortunate when people allow themselves to get like concrete – all mixed up and permanently set.

Well done is better than well said.
Benjamin Franklin

Your attitude is the outward expression
of an inward feeling.

John Maxwell

Dread disease is the
hardening of the attitude.

Success or failure in business is
caused more by the mental attitude
than by mental capacities.

Man creates his environment –
mental, emotional, and physical –
by the attitude he develops.

Life is either a daring adventure or nothing.

Helen Keller

We are either the masters or
the victims of our attitudes.
It is a matter of personal choice –
blessing or curse.

Every change in human attitude must come
through internal understanding
and acceptance. Man is the only
known creature who can reshape
and remold himself by
altering his attitude.

John Maxwell

Always do more
than is required of you.
General George S. Patton

Don't find fault. Find a remedy.
Henry Ford

A positive mental attitude is rooted in clear, calm, and honest self-confidence.

Every problem has in it the seeds
of its own solution. If you don't
have any problems,
you don't get any seeds.

Norman Vincent Peale

You are where you are and what you are
because of the dominating thoughts that
occupy your mind.

John Maxwell

Do you see the green near every sand trap,
or the sand traps around every green?

The situation you live in
doesn't have to live in you.
Roberta Flack

The good news is that the bad news
can be turned into good news
when you change your attitude.
Robert Schuller

Our children are like mirrors – they reflect
our attitudes in life.

Attitude is the criterion for success.
But you can't buy an attitude
for a million dollars.
Attitudes are not for sale.

Denis Waitley

The higher you go in any organization of value, the better the attitude you'll find.

John Maxwell

Man who say it cannot be done should not interrupt man doing it.

Chinese proverb

Beware of those who stand aloof and greet each venture with reproof; the world would stop if things were run by men who say, "It can't be done."

There is no sadder sight
than a young pessimist.
Mark Twain

We are confronted with
insurmountable opportunities.
Pogo (by Walt Kelly)

Never accept the negative
until you have thoroughly
explored the positive.

A person cannot travel within
and stand still without.

James Allen

Nothing will be attempted if all possible
obstacles must first be removed.

Samuel Johnson

My great concern is not whether you have failed, but whether you are content with your failures.

Abraham Lincoln

When you affirm big, believe big, and
pray big, big things happen.
Norman Vincent Peale

We cannot tailor make the situations of our
life, but we can tailor make the attitudes to
fit them before they arrive.

Failure isn't failure unless you don't learn from it.

Dr. Ronald Niednagel

Every success I know has been reached
because the person was able to
analyze defeat and actually profit
from it in the next undertaking.

William Marston

Laughter is the shortest distance
between two people.

Victor Borge

If you have a will to win, you have
achieved half your success;
if you don't, you have achieved
half your failure.

David Ambrose

Life is ten percent how we make it; ninety percent how we take it.

Circumstances do not make you what you are . . . they reveal what you are!

John Maxwell

You can get everything in life you
want if you help enough other people
get what they want.

Zig Ziglar

Of all the things you wear, your expression is the most important.

Failure isn't failure unless you don't learn from it.

Dr. Ronald Niednagel

Ninety-nine percent of failures
come from people who have
the habit of making excuses.
George Washington Carver

It is what you learn after
you know it all that counts.

John Wooden

Lord, grant that I may always desire more
than I can accomplish.

Michelangelo

Again and again, the impossible
problem is solved when we see
that the problem is only a tough
decision waiting to be made.

Robert Schuller

You're more likely to act yourself into feeling, than feel yourself into action.

Psychologist Jerome Bruner

Many intelligent people never move beyond the boundaries of their self-imposed limitations.

John Maxwell

Always help people increase their
own self-esteem. Develop your skill
in making other people
feel important.
Donald Laird

Events are less important
than our responses to them.

John Hersey

When opportunity knocks,
a grumbler complains about the noise.

I got a simple rule about everybody.
If you don't treat me right –
shame on you!
Louis Armstrong

Any manager who can't get along with
a .400 hitter is crazy.

Joe McCarthy, New York Yankees

Always make others feel needed,
important, and appreciated and
they'll return the same to you.

John Maxwell

An optimist is a driver who thinks that empty space at the curb won't have a hydrant beside it.

Changing Times

Optimism is the cheerful frame of mind that enables a teakettle to sing, though in hot water up to its nose.

A pessimist is one who makes difficulties of his opportunities; an optimist is one who makes opportunities of his difficulties.

Reginald B. Mansell

When one door closes, another opens;
but we often look so long and so regretfully
upon the closed door that we do not see
the one which has opened for us.
Alexander Graham Bell

Think right, act right; it is what you think
and do that makes you what you are.

Your attitude speaks so loudly that I can't
hear what you say.

Some people look at things as they are and say, "Why?" I look at things as they can be and say, "Why not?"

Robert Kennedy

Your problem is not your problem.
Your attitude – how you handle
your problems – is your problem.

John Maxwell

The greatest mistake one can make in life is
to be continually fearing you will make one.

Elbert Hubbard

Each day we need good thoughts to
live by. And remember . . .
you get what you order in life.
Alfred A. Montapert

Instead of giving people a piece of your mind, give them a piece of your positive attitude.

To the discontented man no chair is easy.

Benjamin Franklin

A difficult crisis can be more readily endured if we retain the conviction that our existence holds a purpose – a cause to pursue, a person to love, a goal to achieve.

John Maxwell

If you can't fight
and you can't flee . . . flow.

Robert Eliot

Worry does not help anything,
but it hurts everything.

General George S. Patton

Become a possibilitarian. No matter how dark things seem to be or actually are, raise your sights and see possibilities – always see them, for they're always there.

Norman Vincent Peale

Our attitude at the beginning of a task will affect its outcome more than anything else.

John Maxwell

Unless a man undertakes more than he possibly can do, he will never do all he can do.

Henry Drummond

Coaches who can outline plays on a blackboard are a dime a dozen. The ones who win get inside their players and motivate.

It doesn't pay to worry. If you went through last
year's files marked "important,"
chances are the only things you'd keep
are the paper clips.

Robert Orben

Success is going from failure to failure without
loss of enthusiasm.

Abraham Lincoln

My attitude has always been . .
if it's worth playing, it's worth
paying the price to win.

Paul "Bear" Bryant

The person interested in success has to learn
to view failure as a healthy, inevitable part
of the process of getting to the top.

Dr. Joyce Brothers

We tend to get what we expect.

Norman Vincent Peale

The human spirit is never finished
when it is defeated . . .
it is finished when it surrenders.

Ben Stein

The man who goes farthest is generally the one who is willing to do and dare. The sure-thing boat never gets far from the shore.

Dale Carnegie

Most people are very close to becoming the person God wants them to be.

John Maxwell

Leadership has less to do with
position than it does
with disposition.

127

Psychosclerosis: the hardening of the attitude which causes a person to cease dreaming, seeing, thinking, and leading.

Ashley Montague

We cannot hold a torch to light another's path without brightening our own.

Ben Sweetland

Before a person can achieve the kind
of life he wants, he must think, act,
walk, talk, and conduct himself in
all of his affairs as would the person
he wishes to become.

Zig Ziglar

Those folks who succeed simply remain
enthusiastic longer than those who fail.

Ralph Waldo Emerson

We make a living by what we get, but we
make a life by what we give.

Winston Churchill

Winners concentrate on winning; losers concentrate on getting by.

John Maxwell

Any fact facing us is not as important as our attitude toward it, for that determines our success or failure.

Norman Vincent Peale

People who never do any more than they get paid for, never get paid for any more than they do.

An optimist sees an opportunity
in every calamity;
A pessimist sees a calamity
in every opportunity.
Herbert V. Prochnow

It is your actions and attitude when you are on your own that reflect what you really are.

Martin Vanbee

Attitudes are nothing more than habits of thought . . . and habits can be acquired.

Paul J. Meyer

Our attitude toward life determines life's attitude toward us.
John Maxwell

Your attitude tells the world what you can expect from life.

Nothing can stop the person with the right attitude from pursuing his goal.

Ability is what you're capable
of doing. Motivation determines
what you do. Attitude determines
how well you do it.

Lou Holtz

Ninety percent of all those who fail are not
actually defeated . . . they simply quit.

Paul J. Meyer

Start a crusade in your life
to be your very best.

William Danforth

Enthusiasm and persistence can make an average person superior; indifference and lethargy can make a superior person average.

William Ward

It's not where you start –
It's where you finish that counts.

Zig Ziglar

All looks yellow to the jaundiced eye.

Alexander Pope

There is little difference in people,
but that little difference makes a big
difference. The little difference
is attitude. The big difference is
whether it is positive or negative.

Clement Stone

Gratitude is the least of virtues;
but ingratitude the worst of vices.

Two men looked through prison
bars – one saw mud, the
other stars.

[It is] tragic when we put off living. We dream of a magical rose garden over the horizon and miss the roses blooming outside our windows.

Dale Carnegie

Do a little more each day than
you think you possibly can.
Lowell Thomas

Superiority – doing things a little better
than anybody else can do them.
Orison Swett Marden

Chance favors the
prepared mind.
Louis Pasteur

True greatness consists in being
great in little things.

Charles Simmons

We are what we repeatedly do.
Excellence, then, is not an act
but a habit.

Since your thinking has a direct
bearing on your performance,
your thinking must be based on
sound input.
Zig Ziglar

Commitment:
Another name for success.

The only alternative
to perseverance is failure.

I don't know what your destiny will be,
but one thing I know: the only ones
among you who will be really happy
are those who will have
sought and found how to serve.

Albert Schweitzer

There is always a best way of
doing everything.
Ralph Waldo Emerson

Nothing would be done at all if a man
waited until he could do it so well that
no one could find fault with it.
Cardinal Newman

If thinking is viewed as a skill. . .
it can be improved by practice,
as we improve other skills.

I started where the last man left off.
Thomas Edison

I can do small things in a great way.
James Freeman Clarke

Anybody who accepts mediocrity – in school, on the job, in life – is a person who compromises, and when the leader compromises, the whole organization compromises.

Charles Knight

Behind every great idea is someone saying,
"It won't work."

Great things are not done by impulse
but by a series of small things
brought together.

There is no speed limit
in the pursuit
of excellence.

Progress is not created by
contented people.

F. Tyger

I do the very best I know how –
the very best I can; and I mean to keep
on doing so until the end.

Abraham Lincoln

The greatest reward for doing
is the opportunity
to do more.
Jonas Salk

Dr. John C. Maxwell is known across the world as a motivator, encourager and equipper of leaders. He has conducted leadership seminars nationally and internationally, and is the founder and director of INJOY, Inc., a leadership development company. He is the author of seven books published by Thomas Nelson, Victor Books and two titles by Honor Books.